HOW OUR CHOICES IMPACT EARTH™

NONRENEWABLE RESOURCES AND YOU

**NICHOLAS FAULKNER
AND PAULA JOHANSON**

rosen publishing's
rosen
central®

New York

Published in 2019 by The Rosen Publishing Group, Inc.
29 East 21st Street, New York, NY 10010

Copyright © 2019 by The Rosen Publishing Group, Inc.

First Edition

All rights reserved. No part of this book may be reproduced in any form without permission in writing from the publisher, except by a reviewer.

Library of Congress Cataloging-in-Publication Data

Names: Faulkner, Nicholas, author. | Johanson, Paula, author
Title: Nonrenewable resources and you / Nicholas Faulkner and Paula Johanson.
Description: New York : Rosen Central, 2019. | Series: How our choices impact earth | Includes bibliographical references and index. | Audience: Grades 5–8.
Identifiers: LCCN 2017050366| ISBN 9781508181507 (library bound) | ISBN 9781508181514 (pbk.)
Subjects: LCSH: Conservation of natural resources—Juvenile literature. | Nonrenewable natural resources—Juvenile literature. | Materials—Juvenile literature. | Power resources—Juvenile literature.
Classification: LCC HC85 .F383 2019 | DDC 333.8/2—dc23
LC record available at https://lccn.loc.gov/2017050366

Manufactured in the United States of America

CONTENTS

INTRODUCTION — 4

CHAPTER ONE
NONRENEWABLE RESOURCES AND OUR PRODUCTS — 7

CHAPTER TWO
TAPPING ENERGY FROM THE EARTH — 18

CHAPTER THREE
THE CONSEQUENCES OF OUR ACTIONS — 31

CHAPTER FOUR
SMARTER CHOICES — 42

GLOSSARY — 53
FOR MORE INFORMATION — 54
FOR FURTHER READING — 56
BIBLIOGRAPHY — 58
INDEX — 62

INTRODUCTION

Nonrenewable resources are those natural resources we use that won't be replenished by mother nature for a very long time. Fossil fuels, such as oil, natural gas, and coal, are examples of nonrenewable resources. We use oil to produce gasoline and other fuels that power our cars and heat our homes. The reason why fossil fuels are considered nonrenewable is that they come from the remains of plants and animals that have accumulated over millions of years. Since it took millions of years to create these fossil fuels, it will take millions more to replenish them if and when they run out.

Humans have always used natural resources to change the world around them. The first kinds of resources were probably a sharp stick to dig for roots, an animal fur to keep warm in the winter, and a pile of dry grass to cushion a baby's cradle. The oldest signs and tools left by people living long ago are rocks. These were rocks that fit into someone's hand and were broken to have a sharp edge. People living today can trace the scratches made with these rocks on stone and bone.

Today, however, humans are using many more natural resources. One of the effects of using these fossil fuels is the release of carbon into the atmosphere. By 2030, the International Energy Agency (IEA) estimates that humans will have released approximately 1,000 gigatons (907 metric gigatons) of carbon. This is cause for alarm. As of 2015, "U.S. greenhouse gas emissions totaled 7,260 million tons (6,587 million metric tons) of carbon dioxide equivalents," according to the EPA.

Oil-drilling rigs work nonstop to extract fossil fuels from the ground. Eventually, those resources will run out.

The effects on local and global climate are disastrous and still being measured.

The evidence left behind by people living today will last longer than the Egyptian stone statue called the Great Sphinx of Giza, which is ten thousand or more years old. But the signs being left behind will not be whole works of art in thousands of years. The Statue of Liberty and the Golden Gate Bridge will be crumbles of corroded metal. Burnt fossil fuels leave behind polluted air and oceans that will still cause lung and heart illnesses and cancer in the future. Buried radioactive waste will be still dangerous for thousands of years to come.

Now that we know the effects of using our natural resources, we have the power of choice. We can choose to live more sustainably, opting for renewable sources of energy, such as solar and wind, instead of relying on fossil fuels. As consumers, we can choose to buy products that are made in the most Earth-friendly way possible. Collectively, our choices can truly change the world.

CHAPTER ONE

NONRENEWABLE RESOURCES AND OUR PRODUCTS

Today, society as a whole generally values the importance of protecting the environment. More than ever, people all over the world are making the effort to save our natural resources. However, things weren't always this way. The use of natural resources in Western nations began to change after the Renaissance in Western Europe, even before the Industrial Revolution. Businessmen and political leaders no longer thought of people as part of the natural world. It became traditional to view the world's resources and all non-human life as things for people to use up. Natural resources were considered different from capital, which was a term for human-made goods and products.

A more modern approach to resource use is emerging. Economists now view many natural resources as a form of natural capital because they can be made better or worse by human action. The world's natural resources give living beings air and water, as well as food and shelter. The attitude that calls these resources natural capital recognizes that a healthy ecology has value to people. It's not enough just to count the money

NONRENEWABLE RESOURCES AND YOU

Nothing has more value to humanity than Earth's vast resources, such as the forests. Exploiting these resources will cost us dearly in the long term.

that people earn by using a natural resource. When people are aware of any changes they are making to the ecology, they are considerate of its value.

RESPECTING MOTHER EARTH

Ecuador is the first country to pass a law recognizing the rights of nature, which states: "Natural communities and ecosystems possess the unalienable right to exist, flourish, and evolve within Ecuador. Those rights shall be self-executing, and it shall be the duty and right of all Ecuadorian governments, communities, and individuals to enforce those rights." In plain talk, this means that the natural world is protected by law in Ecuador, and all citizens must enforce that law.

In most countries around the world, nature is treated as property under the law. Except for Ecuador's laws, efforts to protect natural resources treat ecosystems as private property or common property. Even the best environmental laws are all written to benefit the interests of property and commerce.

It's not so unusual to recognize the rights of nature. After all, some laws protect farm animals and pets. There are hunting laws to protect wild animals. Rare or endangered plants and animals are protected under state and federal laws. In Canada, many cities protect heritage trees (old-growth trees). New York State even enacted the Bruce S. Kershner Heritage Tree Preservation and Protection Act in 2008 to protect old-growth trees on state land. Other U.S. states have proposed similar laws.

Rights of nature in the constitution of a country can protect ecosystems and communities from development projects that would ruin them. Ecuador's law means that local people and government agencies will make democratic decisions instead of letting corporations compete to exploit natural areas.

AN UNEXPECTED RESOURCE

Nonrenewable resources are not only energy sources. People use a variety of nonrenewable resources for making many products. For some products, it's very easy to tell what resources were used. Gold jewelry has a color different from other metals, for example. For other products, such as plastics, the petroleum resources used are not obvious.

One resource that most people don't realize is nonrenewable is clay. All of the clay in the world is formed by natural geological processes over hundreds of thousands—or millions—of years. Clay has many uses. Sometimes, it is an important ingredient in a product. For other products, clay is used to help process raw materials. Large quantities of china clay (also known as kaolin) are used when making cotton fibers into thread and weaving it into fabric. You may not be able to see clay in laundry products, pencils, or treated sewage, but it's there.

A use for clay that is not commonly known is as a filler. Clay fillers are used in a range of products. For agriculture, clay adds bulk to insecticides and makes nonstick coating for fertilizer pellets. Clay is an important part of many construction products, such as linoleum and cement, as well as paint and enamel. Toothpaste and cosmetics contain clay. Plastics like polypropylene and polyvinyl chloride (PVC) have clay added. Even flour sometimes has clay added.

NONRENEWABLE RESOURCES AND OUR PRODUCTS | 11

Kaolin clay, also known as china clay, is an essential ingredient in the manufacture of china and porcelain. It is also widely used in the making of paper, rubber, paint, and many other products.

There are three kinds of products where the clay content is most obvious or essential: pottery, bricks, and printing. Each of these products uses this nonrenewable resource for different purposes. These three products make good examples of how different planning is needed for each way that a nonrenewable resource is used.

A CONNECTED WEB OF RESOURCES

Interestingly, when clay becomes scarce in a country, the cost of making paper will increase. There is just as much wood to make paper from, after all. But there are other questions to consider. There may not be enough railway cars to ship the needed clay, not without causing problems in shipping the country's grain harvests.

When any one nonrenewable resource runs out, the use of many other resources is affected. Mining metal ores would be done very slowly without the use of machines run on fossil fuels, for example. Some nonrenewable resources are abundant. Others are rare and prized, such as diamonds.

The use of a resource can have unexpected effects. When fuel is distilled from petroleum, there are a lot of waste products. From this waste, plastics and chemical fertilizers are made so that completely new industries have been created using these toxic byproducts. But these materials have lasting bad effects in landfills and croplands, harming both human health and the environment.

POTTERY

People have used clay for pottery since Paleolithic times—for twenty thousand years or more in some parts of the world. When you think of clay, you probably think of china dishes. Or, perhaps you think of modeling clay for sculpting. Kaolin clay makes fine porcelain. In England alone, 1.1 million tons (about 1 million metric tons) of kaolin clay, or about one-third of the china clay used, goes into the making of fine porcelain each year.

For pottery, the clay is shaped and then fired by baking it in a hot oven called a kiln. Usually, the pottery is covered with a glaze made of water, clay, and powdered minerals. It is then fired again. Kilns can be fueled with wood, fossil fuels, or powered with electricity. The temperatures reached are hot enough to melt glass and many metals.

Pottery is hard and brittle. Broken pottery pieces are sharp and have few uses. Spanish architect Antoní Gaudi was able to use broken pottery to make mosaics on several of his buildings. Pieces of broken pottery thousands of years old have turned up in old garbage in many places around the world.

BRICKS

The making of bricks and tiles for the construction industry is really a kind of pottery. But sculptures and dishes are not made from the same clay as bricks and floor tiles. The fine-grained white kaolin clay that makes good plates and figurines would be too hard and brittle for floor tiles or bricks. Instead, coarser clay is mixed with sand and powdered minerals. The resulting bricks and tiles are relatively softer than dishes but are more able to last under the stresses in a building. A brick is porous, almost like a sponge, compared with a bone china teacup.

Cheap, temporary bricks can be dried in sunshine in a hot climate. Some of these cheaper bricks have mud or cow dung mixed into the clay. But for buildings that will last, most bricks are fired in large industrial kilns. The fuel can be wood or charcoal. But in China, it is usually coal. The clay brick industry is a major source

NONRENEWABLE RESOURCES AND OUR PRODUCTS | 15

Bricks are all around us, used in the construction of houses and buildings. Many people don't realize they're made from a nonrenewable resource.

of air pollution in developing countries. The United Nations (UN) and the International Energy Agency are working to encourage all countries to control air pollution.

Another major source of air pollution in developing countries is the making of concrete and concrete bricks, which also contain clay. At least 1 ton (0.9 metric ton) of carbon dioxide gas is released for every ton of concrete made. The smoke from fossil fuels and carbon dioxide are greenhouse gases. These gases are believed, by many scientists, to be causing Earth's atmosphere to be warming up like a greenhouse and causing global climate change.

PAPERMAKING

Still more clay, usually kaolin, is used in papermaking. Paper is made with wood fibers that are cooked into pulp. Clay is mixed into the pulp to give strength and smoothness to many kinds of paper. Without clay, large paper mills would not be able to use machines to make paper. When clay is mixed into the wet slurry of wood fibers, the paper dries tough enough to wind in big rolls to be pulled through large printing presses. Clay also fills in gaps between fibers so that the paper is smooth. It's hard to print with ink on paper that has a rough texture like handmade paper.

Clay is also used as a surface coating that is particularly good for glossy magazines. The result is a smooth surface that takes images well. But the high

NONRENEWABLE RESOURCES AND OUR PRODUCTS | 17

Every time we read a book or write a letter, we're using the natural resources in paper that can take decades, if not hundreds or thousands of years to regenerate.

content of clay makes the glossy paper unrecyclable. Newsprint usually has about 8 percent clay, while magazines can contain up to 30 percent. Un-recycled paper will eventually compost in a garbage dump, but the clay is unrecoverable.

CHAPTER TWO

TAPPING ENERGY FROM THE EARTH

When you flip on a light switch, ride in a car, or charge your smartphone, the energy fueling those actions likely comes from beneath your feet. Underground, in fact. Many of our natural resources are minerals found in the earth. These useful minerals are nonrenewable resources.

Geologists study the rock formations on and under the surface of the earth, learning about the minerals that can be found. People dig mines, boring into mountains or deep into the ground. They look for ores to make metal, or stone that is good for making concrete and buildings. Another reason for mining and drilling holes deep into the ground is to find mineral deposits that can be burned.

Thousands of years ago, people first started burning wood as fuel, using fire to cook food and make tools. People noticed that some black rocks can catch fire and burn hotter than wood. In English, "coal" is a word for both this kind of black rock and for hot, burning pieces of wood. In the Middle East, there are a few places where tarry oil oozes out of the ground or floats to the top of a lake. This is petroleum, from the Greek

TAPPING ENERGY FROM THE EARTH | 19

Coal is a natural resource that people have used for thousands of years. Not only is it nonrenewable, it is also a producer of greenhouse gases.

word for rock oil. Lightning striking the ground can start fires in coal beds and petroleum. In Turkey, near the village of Çirali, natural gas seeps up through cracks in the ground and bursts into flame. People learned to use whatever fuel was available, especially where there are few trees for wood.

There are uses for fire besides getting heat to cook food or smelting metals out of ores. Fuels are burned not only for heating something directly. Fuels are also burned to use the heat to power machines.

Hot air rises. Hot water rises, too. The heat from a fire can be used to move water in a tank and pipes. The moving water can turn the blades of a fan or turbine just like the blades of a windmill turn on a windy day. Once the turbine is turning, it can turn an electric generator. The generator makes electricity.

Another way that burning fuel is used to power machines is in an internal combustion engine, such as the engines in most cars and trucks. The fuel burns inside the engine, making small, controlled explosions of hot gases. The hot gases push the moving parts of the engine.

If you've ever turned an eggbeater by hand, or paddled a boat, you know that it takes a lot of energy to move objects around. Riding a bicycle takes some work. It is much harder to use bike pedals to try to move a large, heavy load. Many inventors have made machines that use burning fuels as a source of energy to do work. These fuels are a good source of energy. There are two kinds of energy sources from nonrenewable resources: fossil fuels and radioactive energy sources.

FUEL FROM FOSSILS

The word "fossil" is from the Latin word *fossilis*, meaning something that has been dug up out of the ground. A fossil is a trace in stone of something that was once living. Over thousands and millions of years, mud and sand can harden into stone and show traces of plants and animals that lived long ago. The trace could be bones from a dinosaur. It could be marks left in mud when leaves fell from trees and plants. A fossil could even be a track of footprints left by an animal running across a riverbank.

The term "fossil fuels" is used for mineral deposits like crude oil or petroleum, natural gas, and coal. Crude oil is a liquid fuel, natural gas is a gaseous fuel, and coal is a solid fuel. Each of these mineral deposits can be burned as a fuel, and it is found by digging or drilling in the ground.

These mineral deposits are believed by most geologists to be formed from plants and animals that were buried hundreds of millions of years ago. In time, mud and rock covering the organic layer would cause heat and pressure. Natural gas and crude oil are the remains of ocean life such as plankton and algae. Coal is the remains of ancient swamps and forests. There are a few scientists, such as Thomas Gold, who believe that these fossil fuels were not organic, or created from living things. Gold said that when the planets of the solar system formed, Earth had a great deal of oil-bearing rock deep around its core. Even if that theory were correct, most of that fossil fuel would be far too deep ever to be used. Only a small amount of oil and gas has come upward through cracks, where people have found it.

Peat is also considered a fossil fuel. Over thousands of years, marsh plants gradually build up and compress to form peat. It is not millions of years old, though. Most peat forms in bogs. People use spades to dig up blocks of peat. When any remaining water has drained out of the blocks, peat can be burned like sticks of firewood. Household stoves and fireplaces in northern Europe used up most of the peat bogs. Since the invention of furnaces that use oil, gas, or electricity, peat is used mostly in gardening as a fertilizer.

FINDING ENERGY IN RADIOACTIVE MATERIALS

There are other minerals that only have been found to be useful since the end of the nineteenth century. Pitchblende, an ore of metal that is heavier than lead, can be found in granite rocks, too. It is a source of uranium. Many chemists, such as Marie and Pierre Curie and Ernest Rutherford, studied uranium and other elements that they found in pitchblende. These studies revealed much about the way matter is made. Atoms of uranium and some other elements release particles that radiate out and interact with other atoms nearby. Marie Curie named this action radioactivity.

Curie observed an interesting quality about radioactive elements like radium. If you get enough of the radioactive element in a lump, it is warmer than its surroundings. In an hour, 1 gram (or 0.035 of an ounce) of radium can melt its own weight in ice. The radioactivity is what causes the heat. Earth's core is hot from the heat made by radioactive elements.

This heat can be useful. In 1942, Enrico Fermi was the first to make what he called an atomic pile. When a pile is carefully made of pellets of uranium formed into rods, separated by control rods of carbon, the radiation increases to a critical point. Carbon rods can be removed or inserted to control the nuclear reaction. The radiation can be used to change atoms within the pile to other elements. The heat of the reaction can be used if the pile is submerged in water.

Here, uranium is being loaded into the reactor pool of the Flamanville Nuclear Power Plant in Flamanville, France.

A modern nuclear reactor in an electrical power plant uses uranium pellets to heat water. The hot water is then used to turn turbines for electric generators. Smaller nuclear reactors with a different design are installed in submarines and large ships to generate electricity. Several space probes, such as *Galileo* and *Cassini*, have cameras and radios powered with small nuclear reactors.

The uranium fuel in a nuclear power plant is effective for only a while. Then, it needs to be removed and replaced. So do the carbon rods and other parts of the reactor. The used, or spent, fuel rods will remain radioactive for tens of thousands of years. The radiation is dangerous, causing harmful changes to cells in living organisms. There is temporary storage for spent fuel rods near most nuclear reactors, in carefully maintained pools of water and boric acid. Reinforced concrete bunkers are also used.

A permanent way to store spent fuel rods is being designed. Sealed containers of spent fuel rods will be buried more than 1,500 feet (450 meters) underground. Geologists are selecting storage sites that have little or no groundwater. There should also be no active earthquake faults nearby.

NUCLEAR THREAT

As the atomic pile or nuclear reactor was being invented, another use for radioactive material was

MANY USES

Natural resources such as coal, natural gas, and petroleum, are good for more than just fuel. These are complex mixtures of organic materials. Over time, they have been changed by heat and pressure into mixtures of substances that have many uses. Some of these substances have unique uses for industry, making crystals and chemicals.

If coal were used only as a fuel, no one would ever have discovered the many useful substances in it. One substance is aniline (also called phenylamine or aminobenzene). In 1856, William Henry Perkin was experimenting with coal, trying to discover a replacement for quinine, which is obtained from the bark of the cinchona tree and is used in medicines. Working with coal tar, he distilled out a substance that made a purple smear. He discovered the first artificial dye.

Perkin's search for a useful medicine in coal tar was a reasonable goal. Aniline is similar chemically to modern painkillers like acetaminophen and to sulfa drugs that cure infections. There are many kinds of medication and hospital supplies made from fossil fuels. When coal is being burned by the railway-car load in power plants, it's not just fuel that is burning. Electricity can be made in many ways, but some medicines and medical equipment can be made only from fossil fuels.

being invented at the same time. Nuclear weapons bring together a critical mass of radioactive material without any carbon rods to slow down and control the reaction. The result is an explosion and scattering of radioactive particles. The force of the explosion is many times greater than for weapons made using fossil fuels. The United States used two nuclear weapons at the end of World War II (1939–1945) in Hiroshima and Nagasaki, Japan.

Many countries around the world, and the United Nations, are working hard to try to ensure that nuclear weapons are never used again in war. Part of this effort is the careful storage of spent nuclear fuel from nuclear reactors so that none of it is lost or stolen. The spent fuel can be used to make nuclear weapons.

WASTED ENERGY

Tens of thousands of oil wells produce hot water as well as crude oil. The water is usually between 250 and 300 °Fahrenheit (120 and 150 °Celsius). The hot water is considered a nuisance. It's usually salty. It has to be separated and dumped, adding about $4 per barrel to the cost of oil.

"The wasted energy in that hot water is the equivalent of the power produced by ten nuclear power plants, according to energy consultant Bernie Karl. In the book *Earth: The Sequel*, Karl is quoted as standing before a roomful of oil and utility executives on more than one occasion and telling them, "You should be ashamed."

Natural gas wells often have a flare, or flame, to burn gas that cannot be processed or sold. Sometimes, the flare burns off "sour gases," which are contaminants like hydrogen sulfide and carbon dioxide. Flaring gets rid of the explosive waste gas and reduces pollution. A flare makes the worksite safer, but it does not put the energy from burning the waste gas to any use.

Flaring is not just a temporary measure. Some flares near Edmonton in Canada have burned for thirty years or more. Gas companies almost never use the waste gas to generate heat or as an energy source. The waste gas is corrosive and ruins pipes.

Similar flares are sometimes necessary at garbage dumps and landfills. Explosive methane gas collects from rotting garbage. On occasion, the methane is burned in flares to get rid of it. A few landfills collect the methane and use it as fuel to burn garbage in an incinerator. The methane is "dirty fuel" with contaminants, but there is less pollution from the incinerator than from just letting the methane leak out of the landfill.

There are many opportunities to use energy instead of wasting it. In his book *The Coming Economic Collapse*, Stephen Leeb wrote of cultural problems with nonrenewable resources. In many cultures around the world, people expect to use resources in the same ways that local people always have. But in India, China, and many African countries, some areas have been cleared almost entirely of trees. People need to walk

28 | NONRENEWABLE RESOURCES AND YOU

This gas flare at an oil refinery in Malaysia burns off gas that is unable to be processed. These flares, and many like them around the world, burn twenty-four hours a day, every day.

for hours each day to find enough wood for fuel to cook a meal. In addition, globalization is bringing modern technology to developing nations. Some corporations expect to use resources and create pollution just as in Western and communist nations.

Leeb calls these expectations "our psychological blind spots: conformity, authority, and groupthink." To Leeb, the biggest obstacle for people today is misplaced priorities. Wanting to own a car does not mean that an oil well's hot water has to be wasted. Wanting to build an electric power plant does not mean that the coal being burned has to make pollution.

MYTHS & FACTS

Myth: People always use up resources and find something new to use up.
Fact: People in many cultures around the world choose to live in a sustainable way within their environments. These cultures use resources in ways that are considerate of the ecology and the needs of future generations. Many aboriginal cultures have sustainable goals, as do the Mennonite, Hutterite, and Amish people of European descent.

Myth: Somebody else will use up that resource, so I might as well get the benefit for my family.
Fact: It is everyone's responsibility to use resources in a way that can sustain a large number of people over a long period of time.

Myth: New resources are accumulating just as they always have.
Fact: Minerals and metals, once mined, are irreplaceable. It takes millions of years for fossil fuel resources like petroleum to form by natural processes. Beds of gravel and clay accumulate during ice ages lasting thousands of years. Even a clear-cut forest needs two to four centuries before it might be possible to harvest fine old-growth timber.

CHAPTER THREE

THE CONSEQUENCES OF OUR ACTIONS

Now that we know the consequences of using up our natural resources, there's good reason to take action and begin living sustainably. However, many people still see natural resources as something to be used up. For them, nonrenewable resources are an opportunity, not a responsibility.

There are also people who take a longer view. Some planners consider what the needs of the community will be in ten years, fifty years, or more. Will there be any of the resource left then, or will only pollution be left? As the population grows older and retires, businesses need to be able to find new workers. When raw materials like marble are shipped to other countries, so are the jobs making marble countertops, rolling pins, and other products. People who live near a resource may end up with no local work opportunities but may do rough physical labor sending raw materials to distant factories. It takes planning to decide how a community can benefit from processing local resources into useful products. It takes consideration to realize how large an area can be affected by resource use.

It can be hard at first to see that there is any choice other than using up an available resource as quickly as possible. Many people work at jobs where nonrenewable resources are gathered and shipped off to distant factories. Speed and efficiency are goals in this kind of work. It's possible to find ways to use a resource without disturbing any more of the environment than necessary. Furthermore, nonrenewable resources provide more opportunities than only service jobs.

A good example of these opportunities is a black rock called argillite. It's found in Haida Gwaii, the Queen Charlotte Islands near the Alaskan panhandle. Haida artists turn argillite into carvings in both modern and traditional styles. Some of the Haida people could easily make a little income selling blocks of argillite from their quarry to rock collector shops across the United States and Canada. But they have decided not to sell uncarved argilite. Their works of art bring far more money to the community than the rough stones ever could.

But a lot happens before carvings leave Haida Gwaii. Artists teaching students their cultural traditions use the stone. Art dealers who market the carvings connect with galleries, museums, and universities to sell these and other artworks. Argillite carving is one part of the cultural renewal in Haida Gwaii. The local economy is supported, as are the traditions. The argillite is not being sold as quickly as possible in rough blocks for distant artists to carve and sell. The nonrenewable resource argillite is being used in a way that sustains the local community.

Sustainable development is the use of resources to meet the needs of the present, without compromising the ability of future generations to meet their own needs. Sustainable development balances the needs of society, the economy, and the environment.

Argillite is mined in Haida Gwaii. The Haida people carve the stone and sell their artwork to sustain the community and respect this nonrenewable resource.

HURTING THE EARTH

When people use nonrenewable resources, there are effects on local ecology. Industry not only creates products—industrial byproducts are also made. Some of these byproducts are waste materials and garbage. Others are air and water pollution. It does people little good to have decent jobs at the mine and mill at their hometown making vermiculite out of asbestos fibers if the fibers sicken many people and farm animals nearby.

An entire biome—a local environment of plants and animals supported by soil, water, and air—can be changed by industry. More than one kind of plant or

NONRENEWABLE RESOURCES AND YOU

animal will suffer when a biome is damaged. Rare plants and animals become endangered or extinct. When people have made a gravel pit or a strip mine, local plants and animals can no longer live in that place.

When people dig out a gravel pit or a limestone quarry, the water drainage for the area is permanently changed. Even if later the topsoil is put back and new trees are planted, the local streams will drain differently on the surface and underground. The change might not look obvious. But that area might no longer be able to support some kinds of plants or the insects

Mining stone not only uses up resources but also impacts the local waterways when runoff collects in the quarries.

and animals that depend on them. The plants that can survive may be like kudzu, a fast-growing weed that chokes trees. The animals that move in may be rats that eat all of the local bird eggs. If there are no birds to eat mosquitoes, people may end up getting malaria from mosquito bites.

People's health is harmed by pollution from factories, power plants, and transporting workers, causing heart and lung diseases and cancer. Wild animals are stressed by noisy industry. Mines produce piles of waste rock called tailings. Rainwater soaks metals and minerals out of tailings to poison streams. Oil wells spill crude oil onto farmers' fields. Burning fossil fuels pollutes the air and water. The oceans and atmosphere are warming, changing weather and natural habitats. Pollution is only one effect, but it is rarely temporary. It can permanently change an area's local ecology, or the entire planet.

DESTROYING RENEWABLE RESOURCES

Some resources renew themselves naturally, such as water or soil or fish. It is important for people to use those resources wisely, instead of using up everything available.

Water moves in a renewing cycle as rain falls from clouds, runs down streams, and evaporates into the air and becomes clouds again. But water is not a renewable resource when people misuse it. Since the 1960s,

ABANDONED COMMUNITIES

There are ghost towns in various places across the United States. A ghost town is a rather eerie place, with empty buildings. Few or no people live where there were once dozens, hundreds, or thousands. One of the most common reasons for people to leave a town is that the resources they relied on when it was built simply aren't there anymore. It takes a network of human activity to support a town. When all of a nonrenewable resource has gone from the town to a larger population center, the town may no longer be supported.

There are a string of ghost towns in the foothills of the Rocky Mountains, along the Brazeau River, where coal was mined in open pits from 1900 to 1960. Mercoal, Robb, and Coal Valley were fine villages with schools and doctors. Cadomin even had stores with women's fashions in 1918. When the coal that was cheap to mine was gone, there was no work. The railway line shut down. Most of the people left these small towns by the early 1960s. Only after 2001 did some developers promote the Coal Branch towns for recreational properties. Other ghost towns have come back from obscurity to be communities of artists and musicians.

THE CONSEQUENCES OF OUR ACTIONS | 37

the Caspian Sea and the Aral Sea in Asia have shrunk to about half their former size. Water from two rivers is being diverted to grow cotton and for industry.

Water can become unusable for drinking or farming. Factory farms are hosed out with clean drinking water.

Though water on Earth seems limitless, its misuse can lead to its disappearance, as we see with the shrinking of the Caspian Sea.

The runoff is full of manure containing germs like *E. coli* 0157:H7, a lethal version of a common germ. The runoff collects in streams, feeding so many algae that fish are smothered. The runoff can get into groundwater and infect people and animals that drink that water.

People can even take water permanently out of the water cycle. Water is injected deep underground into petroleum domes to maintain pressure in oil wells. The water will never come back to the surface and become rain again.

Dirt may seem to be everywhere underfoot. But not all dirt is good for growing plants. When forests are clear-cut, the topsoil may wash away in rainstorms. It takes hundreds of years for new soil to form. If people raise crops without letting farm soil recover, the soil will be less productive. The clear-cutting of forests and overgrazing created the deserts in Lebanon, northern Algeria, and Morocco.

Oceans look huge and seem to have many fish. But people have taken many salmon from the Pacific coast near Washington State and Alaska. There, few salmon are left and the orca whales near Seattle were becoming thin. It's hard for these whales to catch salmon when the Strait of Juan de Fuca has become the world's second-busiest waterway. There's a lot of noise and traffic from hundreds of large ships and small boats. Biologists see this traffic affecting both the fish and the whales. Moreover, commercial fishermen report that the salmon harvest is lower every year.

When people use resources without thinking about the results, many unexpected changes can happen.

THE CONSEQUENCES OF OUR ACTIONS | 39

The Strait of Juan de Fuca has seen a dramatic increase in the amount of boat and ship traffic, which negatively affects the marine life.

Even so-called renewable resources can be used in a way and at a rate that does not allow for natural renewal. These resources are then revealed as nonrenewable resources.

RENEWING PROFITS

It's easy to know the price paid for fuel oil pumped into a tank, ready to fuel a furnace. It's not hard to figure out what part of the price went to pay the trucker's wages.

But the value of the crude oil before it was refined, and who (if anyone) owns that value, is harder to determine. Economists call the value of work and the goods people make capital. Economist Harold Hotelling named some of the values of a natural resource.

In a 1931 article on nonrenewable resource management, Hotelling showed that using up a resource makes it scarcer and increases its price. The maximum price for a resource being exploited is known as Hotelling rent, or scarcity rent.

Scarcity rent is a kind of profit that economists call a resource rent. It is income made not by work but by access to the resource. Using the term "resource rent" is a way that economists recognize natural capital. Natural resources have value that is separate from the work people do.

A person who works should get the income that he or she earns. A person who starts a business should get the income from the business after paying his or her workers. But it's not so clear who should get the profit from using a natural resource. Because nonrenewable resources can be used up, it's important to spend wisely the profit earned by using these resources.

A nation must invest net income from nonrenewable resources in capital to improve its infrastructure, wrote economist John M. Hartwick in 1977. The improvement in lasting buildings, roads, and universities will remain, even as the resource is used up.

Hartwick's rule is being put into use by many nations around the world. The Alaska Permanent Fund was created in 1976 so the state could invest 25 percent of the proceeds from sales of mineral rights like oil and gas. The province of Alberta in Canada created the Heritage Fund in 1970 and contributes a portion of the provincial oil revenues to it. Iceland has a similar fund of its own, but its oil revenues are earned at a higher price per barrel of oil extracted.

CHAPTER FOUR

SMARTER CHOICES

You may think that there's little or nothing you can do to preserve our natural resources, but there is. As a consumer, you have the power of choice. You can choose to buy products that are manufactured in a sustainable way. The first step, though, is to be educated about where your purchases come from. Just because a product is made from materials that are renewable resources does not mean that the product itself is "green," or an environmentally sensible choice. Making the decision of which product to use in a home or work environment can be tricky. There may be factors to think about in ways that are not immediately obvious.

Building construction and renovation are opportunities for making choices about which products to use. The customer, the manufacturer, and the contractor can all be asking themselves about the product and the process being used to make it. But this is why it's important to know which products are made from nonrenewable resources. Many renewable resources are grown using agricultural chemicals and a lot of

SMARTER CHOICES | 43

Using sustainable materials to manufacture products, such as jute fiber to make carpets, is a first step in helping to preserve our resources.

fossil fuels for farm equipment and transportation. If the material of a carpet, for example, is made from renewable jute fiber, that's a good start. The jute could be grown organically without using chemicals. It could also be grown near the factory instead of being shipped overseas.

Ray Anderson is the owner of Interface, a U.S. company that has made carpets since 1976. He was inspired to change his company's methods in 1993. Anderson believed that business "would become more profitable by reducing waste and energy use and its

ALTERNATIVE ENERGY SOURCES

There are other energy sources besides generators run on fossil fuels and radioactive materials. Solar energy systems gather energy from sunlight. Active solar energy systems create electricity when sunlight shines on panels of silicon. Passive solar energy systems collect the heat of sunlight shining on a collector, which can be water or air or a simple wall. Wind energy systems gather energy as the blades or vanes of a windmill turn in the wind to run a water pump or an electric generator. Hydroelectric energy systems use the movement of water to turn an electric generator. Usually, the water is held behind a dam and is carefully released, but there are some turbines in rivers and tidal currents. All of these energy sources are considered alternatives to using fossil fuels and radioactive materials.

An alternative energy source does not use up a nonrenewable resource or create pollution when it generates power. Alternative energy sources are practical ways to make use of the energy freely available from sun, wind, and water. But these alternative energy sources rely on the use of fossil fuels for mining and transportation. Metals and silicon are needed to make solar panels, windmills, and turbines. Great amounts of sand, gravel, and clay need to be moved to make dams. Eventually, most alternative energy sources need to be maintained or replaced. Many of the materials can be recycled or reused.

SMARTER CHOICES | 45

Radioactive materials are good for more than just running power plants. Doctors use radioactive materials for medical imaging in X-ray photographs, CAT scans, and PET scans. Radiation is also used to treat cancer. A few nuclear power plants are designed to create small amounts of materials for medical use. These irreplaceable materials are very radioactive for only a few hours.

Wind turbine farms are a great alternative to nonrenewable energy sources. Wind will always exist and doesn't pollute.

overall impact on the planet," he was quoted in a book by Fred Krupp. "I realized that the way I'd been running my company had been the way of the plunderer."

Anderson's company has reduced water pollution and fossil fuel use. It no longer prints patterns in dyes onto carpet tiles. The machines use loops of yarn to create carpet patterns instead, employing much less water and energy. Their top-selling product mimics the random disorder of a forest floor. There is no pattern to match when laying these carpet tiles, so there is less waste when it is installed. Worn tiles can be replaced without having to tear out an entire carpet. The results inspire Interface's employees and rivals. Greenhouse gas emission for the company has been reduced by 56 percent, while sales have increased by 49 percent.

John Gillespie is a materials expert, landscape designer, and horticulturalist. He said, "One of the keys to building green is getting the design and materials site-specific," according to Tyree Bridge in *BC Homes Magazine*. A good choice for a building on the Atlantic coast might not be as good for a building on the Pacific coast. Gillespie ordered a batch of wool carpet for a house in Vancouver. Wool carpet is made from a renewable resource, sheep's wool. But the raw fleece was shipped from New Zealand to Greece to be spun and woven. The carpet was shipped through England to a Canadian seaport in Halifax, Nova Scotia. From there, the carpet was trucked to Vancouver. "When I figured out the mileage on that carpet, I couldn't believe it," Gillespie said. He was upset by how much fossil fuel was used to transport the wool carpet. "In terms of green, I would have been better to just order something from back east."

YOUR POWER TO MAKE CHANGE

There are many choices you can make about your own use of nonrenewable resources. What you eat, what transportation you use, how you furnish your room—you may have more choices than you think at first.

Because plants and animals replenish naturally, food should be a renewable resource. But most food these days is grown and shipped with the use of fossil fuels. A vegetarian diet uses far fewer fossil fuels than are needed to raise animals for meat. As Alisa Smith and James MacKinnon wrote in their book *Plenty*, the food that Americans and Canadians eat now typically travels between 1,500 and 3,000 miles (2,414 and 4,828 kilometers) from farm to plate. When they learned this statistic, Smith and MacKinnon ate food grown within 100 miles (160 km) of their home for a year.

Their book became a bestseller. The "hundred

Transporting goods is a major contributor to greenhouse gas emissions. Buying foods that are grown and raised locally helps cut down on pollution and the use of fossil fuels.

mile diet" has now become a fun and fashionable way to learn about locally grown food. If not for a year, then for a party or for one day every week, many people are choosing to eat food that has not been transported any farther than one hundred miles.

There are more ways to get around town than by owning a gasoline-powered car. A bicycle is made of much less metal than a car and rolls without fuel. For many people, a bike meets most of their transportation needs. Riding the bus is an alternative that shares the use of fossil fuel among more people. A car-share cooperative lets a group of people share the use of a few cars when needed.

There are other options for cars as well, such as the two-seater Smart Car. The IEA estimates that by 2050, as much as 30 percent of the fuel used for transportation could be biofuel from plants instead of fossil fuels.

Tesla, Inc., is one of the companies that are developing alternative fuel strategies. In addition to manufacturing groundbreaking electric car technology, it also produces solar panels and "Powerwall" batteries to produce energy for the home. In 2017, the company produced its Model 3 electric car, a relatively affordable model that has a range of 220 miles (354 kilometers).

As for furnishing your room or home, there are many choices. Are there any products made by local companies using renewable resources? Perhaps you'll be able to choose a mattress made of latex from rubber trees. A futon made of organic cotton may suit you better. An old bed frame or desk doesn't have to be thrown away. Try a few tightened screws and a little brass polish,

SMARTER CHOICES | **49**

Car2Go is a car-sharing service that exclusively rents fuel-efficient Smart Cars. Eco-friendly services such as these aim to significantly cut greenhouse gas emissions.

wood stain, or paint. You might give old furniture some vintage style or make a personal piece of modern art.

MINDFUL CONSUMPTION

All products used in the United States have ingredient lists and company records. This is so you will know what you are using and how it was made. Read labels. Ask questions when you go into a business. And do internet searches among company websites. You can

NONRENEWABLE RESOURCES AND YOU

find out if the products you want to use are made using nonrenewable resources in a responsible manner.

When you choose to consume nonrenewable resources, do so mindfully. Know where the products you use come from and how they are transported to you. Learn what you can about how the infrastructure of the United States uses up resources at a rate that cannot be sustained. A good way to start is by learning how nonrenewable resources are consumed to make and distribute consumer goods. Then, take that experience to the decisions you make about

Paying attention to labels on the products you buy is a good way to become mindful of how they're produced and with what materials.

essential things like food staples, shelter, energy use, and transportation. There is no one right answer for how nonrenewable resources ought to be used. There are plenty of reasons for any of the decisions you may choose to make.

Even young people can become informed and prepared for making active decisions in all these areas. When you work toward a career or start a business of your own, that's an opportunity to apply what you know about nonrenewable resources.

"USE IT UP, WEAR IT OUT, MAKE IT DO, OR DO WITHOUT."

There was a popular saying when rationing of consumer goods was in place during World War II: "Use it up, wear it out, make it do, or do without." At that time, people couldn't just buy another coat or car or nylon stockings. That attitude doesn't seem old-fashioned in the twenty-first century. It's beginning to become popular again.

The marketing of consumer goods doesn't account for the cost of using up nonrenewable resources. Price tags don't say what part of the price for a product goes to pay for nonrenewable resources. As venture capitalist John Doerr said in *Earth: The Sequel*, "It's really hard to change consumer behavior when consumers don't know how much their behavior costs."

TEN GREAT QUESTIONS
TO ASK YOUR SCIENCE TEACHER

1. How will a nature reserve or national park protect resources as well as biomes?
2. How is electrical power generated?
3. Is this product made by using any recycled materials?
4. What is this product's environmental footprint?
5. How many years' worth of resources are available for making this product in the future?
6. How is the natural capital from this product being spent?
7. What community development programs does this product's manufacturer maintain?
8. What renewable resource alternatives are used when making this product and in the manufacturer's facilities in general?
9. What kind of vehicles are in the manufacturer's transportation fleet, and are these vehicles powered by fossil fuels or alternatives?
10. Does this manufacturer transport materials overseas by boat or by airplane?

GLOSSARY

biome An ecological environment, including plants, animals, water, atmosphere, soil, and minerals.
conformity The action of doing things the same way that other people do.
contaminant An unwanted substance, sometimes dangerous or poisonous, such as hydrogen sulfide mixed into natural gas.
critical mass An amount of radioactive element that releases enough particles to cause a chain reaction that can be sustained.
ecology The study of interactions of organisms with each other and their environment.
greenhouse gas A gas-like carbon dioxide and pollution from burning fossil fuels, which are believed to cause global climate change.
groupthink The effort that people make as a group to try to think the same way for good or bad reasons; a word made up by George Orwell in his book *1984*.
infrastructure A nation's lasting capital, including buildings, roads, utilities, schools and universities, health care, and justice systems.
natural capital The value of a natural resource, particularly a nonrenewable resource; the net profit from the sale of a product after subtracting production costs and fair value for investment.
organic Relating to material made of or by living organisms or once-living organisms.
sustainable development The use of resources to meet the needs of the present, without compromising the ability of future generations to meet their own needs.

FOR MORE INFORMATION

Conservation International
2011 Crystal Drive, Suite 500
Arlington, VA 22202
(800) 429-5660
Website: http://www.conservation.org
With more than 1,000 people and work with more than 2,000 partners in 30 countries, Conservation International has been protecting nature for the benefit of all for nearly 30 years through science, policy, and partnerships with countries, communities and companies.

Energy Information Administration
1000 Independence Ave SW
Washington, DC 20585
(202) 586-8800
Website: http://www.eia.doe.gov
This office serves adults, students, and schoolchildren, providing information on energy data and statistics, in person, online, and by phone. There is a live expert available from 9 am to 5 pm, Eastern Standard Time, from Monday to Friday.

Environment and Climate Change Canada
Public Inquiries Centre
7th floor, Fontaine Building
200 Sacré-Coeur Boulevard
Gatineau QC K1A 0H3 Canada
(800) 668-6767 (in Canada only)
(819) 938-3860
Website: http://www.ec.gc.ca

Environment Canada's mission is to preserve and enhance the quality of Canada's natural environment.

The Nature Conservancy
4245 North Fairfax Drive, Suite 100
Arlington, VA 22203-1606
(703) 841-5300
Website: http://www.nature.org
Founded in 1951, the Nature Conservancy works around the world to protect ecologically important lands and waters for nature and people.

United Nations Department of Economic and Social Affairs
Division for Sustainable Development
Two United Nations Plaza, Room DC2-2220
New York, NY 10017
Email: https://sustainabledevelopment.un.org/contact
Website: https://sustainabledevelopment.un.org
The international organization provides leadership and expertise in sustainable development and monitors program progress.

FOR FURTHER READING

Bloomberg, Michael, and Carl Pope. *Overheated: How Cooler Heads Can Cool the World.* New York, NY: St. Martins Press, 2017.

Gleeson-White, Jane. *Six Capitals, or Can Accountants Save The Planet?: Rethinking Capitalism for the Twenty-First Century.* New York, NY: W.W. Norton & Company, 2015.

Gore, Albert. *Our Choice.* New York, NY: St. Martins Press, 2009.

Grinspoon, David. *Earth in Human Hands: Shaping Our Planets Future.* New York, NY: Grand Central, 2016.

Kolbert, Elizabeth. *The Sixth Extinction: An Unnatural History.* New York, NY: Picador, 2015.

Leonard, Annie, and Ariane Conrad. *The Story of Stuff: The Impact of Overconsumption on the Planet, Our Communities, and Our Health—and How We Can Make It Better.* New York: Free, 2011.

Moss, Stephen. *Planet Earth II.* London, England: BBC Books, 2016.

Ohlson, Kristin. *The Soil Will Save Us!: How Scientists, Farmers, And Foodies are Healing the Soil to Save the Planet.* Emmaus, PA: Rodale, 2014.

Robbins, Jim. *The Man Who Planted Trees: A Story of Lost Groves, The Science of Trees, and a Plan to Save the Planet.* New York, NY: Spiegel & Grau, 2015.

Robinson, Lori. *Wild Lives: Leading Conservationists on the Animals and the Planet They Love.* New York, NY: W. W. Norton, 2017.

Schor, Juliet. *True Wealth: How and Why Millions of Americans Are Creating a Time-Rich, Ecologically Light, Small-Scale, High-Satisfaction Economy.* New York, NY: Penguin, 2010.

Wilson, Edward O. *Half-Earth: Our Planets Fight For Life.* New York, NY: Liveright Publishing Corporation, A Division Of W.W. Norton & Company, 2017.

BIBLIOGRAPHY

Alaska Permanent Fund Corporation. "What Is the Alaska Permanent Fund?" Retrieved October 17, 2008. http://www.apfc.org/home/Content/permFund/aboutPermFund.cfm.

Asheim, Geir B., Wolfgang Buchholtz, John M. Hartwick, Tapan Mitra, and Cees Withagen. "Constant Saving Rates and Quasi-arithmetic Population Growth Under Exhaustible Resource Constraints." *Journal of Environmental Economics and Management*, 53, 2007, pp. 213–239.

Bakan, Joel. *The Corporation: The Pathological Pursuit of Profit and Power*. New York, NY: Free Press, 2004.

Booth, David. "U.S. Giants See Profit in Eco-friendly Autos." *Victoria Times-Colonist,* November 5, 2008, p. B7.

Bridge, Tyee. "The Right Stuff." *BC Homes Magazine*, September/October 2008, pp. 27–28.

Brune, Michael. *Coming Clean: Breaking America's Addiction to Oil and Coal*. San Francisco, CA: Sierra Club Books, 2008.

Caliber Planning. "What Is Flaring?" Retrieved October 28, 2008. https://www.proactiver-fn.com/index.php?content=faq&section=flaring.

Curie, Marie. "Radium and Radioactivity." Marie Curie and the Science of Radioactivity, 2001–2008. Retrieved November 1, 2008. http://www.aip.org/history/curie/article.htm.

Dormer, Wolfgang. "BP's Perspective on Future Fuels." March 18, 2008. http://www.mam.gov.tr/eng/institutes/ee/cnapril2008/sunu/bp.ppt.

Energy Information Administration. "Petroleum Basic Statistics." September 2008. http://www.eia.doe.gov/basics/quickoil.html.

Gold, Thomas. *The Deep Hot Biosphere: The Myth of Fossil Fuels*. New York, NY: Copernicus Books, 2001.

Graham, Ian. *Fossil Fuels: A Resource Our World Depends On*. Chicago, IL: Heinemann Library, 2005.

Hartwick, John M. "Intergenerational Equity and the Investment of Rents from Exhaustible Resources." *American Economic Review*, 67, December 1977, pp. 972–4.

Herbert, John W. "BC's Orcas Suffer Their Worst Die-off in a Decade." *Kayak Yak*, October 26, 2008. http://kayakyak.blogspot.com.

"Inventory of U.S. Greenhouse Gas Emissions and Sinks." EPA. April 14, 2017. https://www.epa.gov/ghgemissions/inventory-us-greenhouse-gas-emissions-and-sinks.

Jaccard, Mark Kenneth. *Sustainable Fossil Fuels: The Unusual Suspect in the Quest for Clean and Enduring Energy*. Cambridge. MA: Cambridge University Press, 2005.

Krupp, Fred, and Miriam Horn. *Earth: The Sequel. The Race to Reinvent Energy and Stop Global Warming*. New York, NY: W. W. Norton & Co., 2008.

Leeb, Stephen, with Glen Strathy. *The Coming Economic Collapse: How You Can Thrive When Oil Costs $200 a Barrel*. New York, NY: Warner Business, 2006.

Morgan, James. "Mud Eruption 'Caused by Drilling.'" *BBC News*, November 1, 2008. http://news.bbc.co.uk/2/hi/science/nature/7699672.stm.

Nonrenewable Energy Sources - Energy Explained, Your Guide To Understanding Energy - Energy Information Administration. Retrieved October 13, 2017. https://www.eia.gov/energyexplained/?page=nonrenewable_home.

O'Carroll, Eoin. "Ecuador Constitution Would Grant Inalienable Rights to Nature." *Christian Science Monitor*'s Bright Green Blog, September 3, 2008. http://features.csmonitor.com/environment/2008/09/03/ecuador-constitution-would-grant-inalienable-rights-to-nature.

Parker, Janine. *The Electron Centennial Page*. Retrieved October 13, 2017. http://www.davidparker.com/janine/electron.html.

Smith, Alisa, and James MacKinnon. *Plenty: One Man, One Woman, and a Raucous Year of Eating Locally*. New York, NY: Random House, 2007.

ThinkQuest. "Nuclear Waste Storage." Retrieved October 20, 2008. http://library.thinkquest.org/17940/texts/nuclear_waste_storage/nuclear_waste_storage.html.

Tomko, Heather. "Ecuador's Constitutional Amendment Will Benefit Environment." *The Tartan*, October 13, 2008. http://www.thetartan.org/2008/10/13/forum/ecuador.

Waters, Bella. *Kazakhstan in Pictures*. Minneapolis, MN: Twenty-First Century Books, 2007.

Weller, Christian E. "Record Gas Prices Add Pressure to Already Squeezed Consumers." *Center for American Progress*, April 22, 2008. http://www.americanprogress.org/issues/2008/04/record_gas_prices.html.

INDEX

A

air pollution, 16
alternative energy sources, 44–45
argillite, 32
atomic pile, 23, 24

B

biome, 33–34, 52

C

capital, 7, 40
carbon, 4, 23, 24, 26
carbon dioxide, 16, 27
clay, 10, 12, 13, 14, 16, 17, 30, 44
  bricks, 13–14, 16
  kaolin clay, 10, 13, 14, 16
  papermaking, 16–17
  pottery, 13
climate, 5, 35
coal, 4, 14, 18, 20, 21, 25, 29, 36
cultural problems, 27, 29
Curie, Marie and Pierre, 22–23

E

energy, 6, 10, 18, 20, 22, 26, 27, 43, 44, 46, 48, 51
environment, ways to protect it, 7, 9
environmental laws, 9

Environmental Protection Agency (EPA), 5

F

fossil fuels, 4, 5, 6, 12, 13, 16, 20, 21, 22, 25, 26, 30, 35, 43, 44, 46, 47, 48, 52
  definition of, 21
  history of, 21

G

gas flare, 27
greenhouse gas, 4, 16, 46

H

Hartwick's rule, 40–41

I

International Energy Agency (IEA), 4, 16, 48

J

jute fiber, 43, 46

L

living sustainably, 31

M

mindful consumption, 49–51
minerals, 12, 18, 44
mining, 12, 18, 44

N

natural capital, 7–8, 40, 52
natural gas, 4, 20, 21, 25, 27
natural resources, 4, 6, 7, 8, 9, 18, 25, 31, 40, 42
  history of use, 7
  saving them, 7
  variety of uses, 25
nonrenewable resources, 4, 10, 12, 18, 20, 27, 31, 32, 33, 36, 39, 40, 42, 44, 47, 50, 51
  effects on local ecology, 33, 34
  making products with, 10
  myths and facts about, 30
nuclear reactors, 24, 26
  storage of used fuel, 24
  use of fuel, 24
nuclear threat, 24, 26

O

oil, 4, 18, 20, 21, 22, 26, 29, 35, 38, 39, 40, 41

P

peat, 22
petroleum, 10, 12, 18, 20, 21, 25, 30, 38
pitchblende, 22
pollution, 16, 27, 29, 31, 33, 35, 44, 46
power of choice, 6, 42
profits, 39–40

R

radioactive materials, 22, 24, 26, 44, 45
rationing, 51
renewable resources, 6, 35, 39, 42, 43, 46, 47, 48, 52
rights of nature, 8–9

S

scarcity rent, 40
sustainable development, 33
sustainable products, choosing, 46–47

U

United Nations, 16, 26

W

water, 7, 13, 20, 22, 24, 26, 29, 33, 34, 35, 37, 38, 44, 46

ABOUT THE AUTHORS

Nicholas Faulkner is a writer living in New Jersey.

For fifteen years, Paula Johanson operated an organic-method market garden, selling produce and sheep's wool at farmers markets. She has written and edited more than twenty nonfiction books on science, health, and literature. At two or more conferences each year, she leads panel discussions on practical science and how it applies to home life and creative work. An accredited teacher, Johanson has written and edited curriculum educational materials for the Alberta Distance Learning Centre in Canada.

PHOTO CREDITS

Cover mikulas1/E+/Getty Images; pp. 4–5 (background) namtipStudio/Shutterstock.com; p. 5 pan demin/Shutterstock.com; pp. 7, 18, 31, 42 Rasta777/Shutterstock.com; p. 8 brave-carp/E+/Getty Images; p. 11 Sinisa Kukic/Moment/Getty Images; pp. 14–15 Lester Lefkowitz/Photographer's Choice/Getty Images; p. 17 Robert Essel NYC/Corbis/Getty Images; p. 19 titop81/iStock/Thinkstock; p. 23 Catherine Pouedras/Science Source; pp. 28–29 hkhtt hj/Shutterstock.com; p. 33 Valery Voennyy/Alamy Stock Photo; p. 34 ollo/E+/Getty Images; p. 37 Anton Balazh/Shutterstock.com; p. 39 Chris Cheadle/All Canada Photos/Getty Images; p. 43 jayk7/Moment/Getty Images; p. 45 thebroker/iStock/Thinkstock; p. 47 majeczka/Shutterstock.com; p. 49 EQRoy/Shutterstock.com; p. 50 Hill Street Studios/Blend Images/Getty Images.

Design: Michael Moy; Photo Research: Karen Huang